Eustace Neville Rolfe, Domenico Monaco

A complete guide to the small bronzes and gems in the

Naples Museum

Eustace Neville Rolfe, Domenico Monaco

A complete guide to the small bronzes and gems in the Naples Museum

ISBN/EAN: 9783337141554

Printed in Europe, USA, Canada, Australia, Japan

Cover: Foto ©Andreas Hilbeck / pixelio.de

More available books at **www.hansebooks.com**

A COMPLETE GUIDE

TO THE

SMALL BRONZES AND GEMS

IN THE

NAPLES MUSEUM,

ACCORDING TO

· THE NEW ARRANGEMENT.

REPRINTED FROM THE COMPLETE HANDBOOK.

THE ORIGINAL WORK BY

DOMENICO MONACO,

CURATOR OF THE MUSEUM;

THE ENGLISH EDITION BY

E. NEVILLE ROLFE, ESQ., B.A.,

HEACHAM HALL, ENGLAND.

LONDON:

PRINTED BY WILLIAM CLOWES AND SONS, Limited,

STAMFORD STREET AND CHARING CROSS.

1883.

THE SMALL BRONZES AND GEMS.

We think a brief summary of the specimens in this collection will be useful to our readers before proceeding to the detailed description.

THE FIRST ROOM.

ARTICLES FOR PUBLIC USE.

Two Curule chairs. Two Bisellia or seats of honour for Proconsuls. The large brazier from the public baths.

ARTICLES FOR RELIGIOUS USES.

Beautiful laver for containing lustral water. The (so-called) tripod of Isis. Vases, cups, craters, and *paterœ* used in worship. A *lectisternium* or bench upon which the images of the gods were placed during the rites. Votive offerings.

HOUSEHOLD CHATTELS.

Braziers, stoves, vases, candelabra, scoops, pails, stools, jugs, and vessels of every kind. Jets and sprays for fountains, bathing apparatus, locks and keys. Tools and agricultural implements; lamps and lanterns.

SECOND ROOM.

Large cork model of the excavations at Pompeii.

Large number of water tanks. Case of bowls, basins, and *paterœ*. Case of funnels, urns, and sundries. Case of portable altars and tables for divinations. Case of weights and measures. Three bedsteads. Glazed tables containing engineering instruments. Fishing-tackle. Musical instruments. *Tesserœ*, or tickets for theatres. Toilet requisites. Surgical instruments. Writing materials. Horse harness and cooking utensils.

THE ROOM OF GEMS.

Articles of silver plate. Gold ornaments in great variety. Magnifying glass. Unique collection of rings, and many hundred cameos and intaglios, some of which are of great celebrity.

B

SMALL BRONZES.

This collection of small bronzes, numbering some thirteen thousand specimens, nearly all found in Pompeii or Herculaneum, is the unique feature of the Naples Museum.

This department never fails to interest the passing visitor, while it is a mine of wealth to the antiquary, as it contains many perfect specimens of the everyday articles of personal use and ornament which eighteen centuries ago were connected with the public and private life of the Roman citizens.

All these articles, from the elaborate curule chair to the most common kitchen utensil, are designed and executed with an artistic grace which reaches the acme of perfection and elegance. Their number alone is sufficient to stock several museums, and such is the elegance of their form and the perfection of their execution that they are no doubt correctly attributed to Greek artists, who alone would be likely to carry their taste for ornament into such minute details.

The difference between the work of these Pompeian artists and that of the artificers of our utilitarian age is especially noticeable in these rooms. Everything in a Roman house displayed the master hand of the artist in an unaffected but quite unmistakable manner; whereas our household chattels, being made to a pattern and in vast numbers, though they answer their purpose admirably, may justly be treated as being the production of a mechanical age, testifying rather to the skill of the artisan than to the taste of the artist.

> The paintings on the walls are of no artistic merit. They represent records of the Farnese family; and battle scenes attributed to Borgognoni.
>
> The asterisk (*) denotes the specimens illustrated in Signor Monaco's large work, and the dagger (†) other noteworthy objects.
>
> Where a Latin word is given in italics, the reader will find an article on the subject in Smith's 'Dictionary of Antiquities.'

FIRST ROOM.

IN THE CENTRE, CLOSE TO THE DOOR, ON AN ANTIQUE MARBLE TABLE,

*72983. *Economic Kitchener* or **Brazier**, in the shape of a rectangular fortress, with four **towers** at the angles. In the centre **is a pan**, in which **the embers** were laid, **the** fire being surrounded ·by a jacket of **water** contained in the **square conduit which** flows beneath the battlements. The water could be drawn off by a tap in one of the sides. Spits for roasting were laid across the embrasures. Thus the kitchener furnished hot water, and was adapted for all other culinary purposes, as well as for heating a room; while the steam from the water neutralized the noxious gases from the charcoal. **Height, 12 in. × 25 in.** broad each side. (*Herculaneum.*)

72984. A rectangular **brazier, with four castors still in** working order. (*Pompeii.*)

72985. TRICLINIUM **on** five feet, on which **the ancients** reclined at meals. **This** one was **made** for only one person. The leather cushion, like all **the** others in this room, is modern, imitated from the antique, which can be done accurately from the impression made in the ashes. Length, 6 ft. Height, **1 ft.** 4 in. (*Pompeii.*)

109831. Brazier with **original ashes** in it. (*Pompeii.*)

UPON A MODERN MARBLE TABLE,

*72986. ECONOMIC **KITCHENER, consisting of** a covered cylindrical boiler, communicating with a hollow semicircle, provided with a tap **to draw** off, the hot water. The fire within the semicircle heated the boiler, and the three swans upon it are constructed **to carry a saucepan.** Roasting could be carried on over **the** brazier in front. **Height** of boiler, 18 in.; diameter, **7 in.** Brazier, **18 in. square.** (*Stabia.*)

†72987. Bronze pedestal **of** a table formed of a rectangular column, surmounted by a bearded head of Bacchus bearing a cup with bracket, intended to support a marble table top. In front of the column a charming "Victory," with flowing robe and holding a martial trophy in her right hand, rests her feet upon **a** globe bearing **a silver**

crescent. Height of column, 33 in.; Victory, 13 in. (Nov. 29, 1864. *Pompeii.*)

111047. Folding table in bronze, with "*semisanto*" marble top. Stands on horses' hoofs and is decorated with horses' heads. The edge of this table is inlaid with silver. Height, 26 in.; width, 20 in. (Feb. 8, 1876. *Pompeii.*)

*72988. BISELLIUM adorned with superb ornamentation in copper. The obverse is decorated with two finely-executed horses' heads, and two human heads with beards. The reverse shows the heads of two geese and two Medusæ. 3 ft. 4 in. × 1 ft. 4 in. (*Pompeii.*)

"The right of using this seat was granted as a mark of honour to distinguished persons by the magistrates and people in provincial towns. The word *bisellium* is not classical, but it occurs in inscriptions."—SMITH, *Dict. Ant.*

72989. Brazier damascened in copper. (*Pompeii.*)

*72990. LAVER (*aqua minarium*) for lustral water. The centro is inlaid with silver and red mastic. Diameter, 2 ft. 10 in., including the edge. (*Temple of Isis, Pompeii.*)

72991. BRAZIER. The obverse and reverse are adorned with Genii, head of Medusa, and two lions' masks. The feet are of griffins. (July 4, 1822. *Pompeii.*)

72992. BISELLIUM adorned with the heads of asses and of men, and designs in silver and copper. On the reverse, the heads of geese and two masks. (*Pompeii.*)

72993. Small tripod on lions' claws for sacrifices. The edge is carefully worked. Height, 13 inches. (*H.*)

72994. FOLDING TABLE. The edging which secures the marble and the four legs with lions' feet are inlaid with silver sprays. These legs have on the upper parts acanthus leaves, from which young Satyrs are emerging, each one holding a rabbit under his arm. (*Pompeii.*)

UNDER GLASS ON A POMPEIAN MOSAIC TABLE,

*72995. SACRIFICIAL TRIPOD, of beautiful execution. Its three lion-footed legs are capped by a seated Sphinx and adorned with beautiful arabesques and bearded heads of Jupiter Ammon. The legs are braced together by elegant sprays of lotus flowers. The basin is adorned with festoons and the skulls of bulls,—emblems which remind us that it was destined to receive the blood of victims. Height, 3 ft. Side of tripod, 21½ inches. Height of basin, 3½ inches. Many guide-books assign this tripod to the Temple of Isis. It was, in fact, found at Herculaneum.

72997. Double iron ring used as stocks. (Lock missing.) Diameter, 2 ft. (*Pompeii.*)

*72998. STOCKS found in the barracks at Pompeii (Acts xvi. 24). Each partition confined the ankle of a prisoner, who was accordingly forced to sit or lie upon the ground. These stocks would secure twenty prisoners, and the extremity of the sliding bar was fastened with a lock. From the nail-holes in the cross-irons we see that the structure was fixed to the floor of the gaol. Four skeletons were found fixed in this terrible instrument, the suddenness of the calamity not permitting of their release. Length, 7 ft. 4 in. (*Pompeii.*)

†111050. Small CHAIR with back; the only specimen yet discovered of its kind. The woodwork is modern, but copied from the carbonised remains of the ancient wood. Height, 1 ft. 9 in.; back, 9 in.; width, 1 ft. 3 in. (February 1876. *Pompeii.*)

UNDER GLASS ON A POMPEIAN MOSAIC TABLE,

*73000. CANDELABRUM formed of a decorated Corinthian column, bearing on the obverse a tragic mask, and on the reverse a "*bucranium*," or skull of a bull. Four branches issue from the top of the column, from which four handsome double-wick lamps hang by four stranded chains. These lamps were not found with the candelabrum and do not belong to it, but they are of fine workmanship. The one decorated with the head of an elephant, and suspended by two dolphins, is unique. Standing upon the left angle of the base upon the elaborate clusters of vine-leaves inlaid in silver, we observe a fine group composed of Acratus (a genius of Bacchus) mounted on a panther, the *rhyton* in his hand, and opposite to him a small altar, upon which burns the sacred fire. Height, 4 ft. 1 in. (*House of Diomede, Pompeii.*)

73003 and 73007. Two baths, the only bronze ones yet discovered. One has a plug-hole in the corner to let off the water and four fluted handles.

†73005. GREAT BRAZIER for use in the public baths, found in the *tepidarium* of the baths near the Temple of Fortune at Pompeii. Its object was to raise the chamber to a gentle temperature, thus preparing the bather for

the hotter chamber. On one side we observe a cow in relief and the words "M. Nicidius P." (*M. Nicidius posuit*), denoting probably that it was his gift. A precisely similar brazier stands in the public baths at Pompeii. Height, 2 ft. 1 in.; length, 8 ft.; width, 2 ft. 9 in.

Behind the brazier,

73017. **Long** four-legged bench from the public **baths.** (*Pompeii.*)

Six Candelabra, adapted to a single lamp. They are telescopic, and constructed to take to pieces in a very ingenious and simple manner. (*Pompeii.*)

Sundry braziers and small altars (square and circular), almost all of them ornamented with carving or reliefs. (*Pompeii* and *Herculaneum.*)

73016. Iron stove, oxidized by *lapilli*. This stove has places for two saucepans, and the bottom is of fire-brick. (*Pompeii.*)

In the centre, immediately behind the *Triclinium*,

*73018. Cylindrical stove (*calidarium*), of exquisite beauty. It stands on three lions' feet and has four handles, of which two are fastened to the sides by models of human hands. On the upper·part are two handles, each of them formed by two wrestlers, whose exertions are portrayed with wonderful realism. The lid is surmounted by a Cupid astride of a dolphin, holding a lyre in his right hand. The interior of this stove is of very peculiar construction, the upper part being a boiler which communicates with the firebars beneath, which are hollow. Two comic masks at the back of the stove form uptakes for the fire, while a third over the stove door communicates with the boiler, and probably was originally furnished with a tap. Height, 3 ft. 6 in.; diameter, 14 in. (May 1863. *Pompeii.*)

This stove stands on

73019. A round marble table, which served as the base of a fountain. The water flowed away through the lions' masks on the edge. (*Herculaneum.*)

73020-1-2. Three safes. All found empty. The centre one, which is of iron, is the finest. Its obverse is adorned with bronze nails and two busts of Diana in relief; between them, the head of a wild boar. Beneath, two busts of Genii of Bacchus, and the mask of a Bacchante. An elegant handle served to raise the lid of this beautiful safe. Height, 36 in.; length, 41 in.; width, 23 in. Found in a room to the right of the *tablinum* of the house of C. Vibius with the bedsteads (see next room). (1867. *P.*)

The safe to the left is also of iron. The obverse is covered with bronze panels framed in iron cornices. This is the only safe with a keyhole, and beneath the keyhole is an image of Jupiter in bas-relief upon a pedestal, and a priestess pouring a libation upon an adjacent altar. (1864. *P.*)

The third safe is entirely of iron. On its obverse are the six following busts in relief:—Minerva, Mercury, Bacchus, Juno, Apollo, Diana, and (on the top of the lid) Jupiter. (1869. *Pompeii.*)

IMMEDIATELY BELOW THE THREE SAFES, STAND

*109983 and 111764. Two LECTISTERNIA, used by the ancients for the Penates and the sacred vessels. They stand on four feet, and their edges are inlaid with waving designs in silver and Greek patterns. The woodwork painted red is a restoration from the old carbonised wood which was found upon them. Height, 14 in.; length, 3 ft. 3 in.; width, 13 in. Found January 1874, at Pompeii.

11232. Bronze fragments of a BEDSTEAD, standing between the two Lectisternia, put up on a short frame merely for purposes of exhibition. (1877. *Pompeii.*)

ON A ROUND MARBLE TABLE,

†109697. BELL-SHAPED VASE, on a quadrangular base. This vase is one of the finest in the collection, especially remarkable for its two handles. These rise above the edge and rest on miniature acanthus leaves, and, curving back gracefully, cling to the sides of the vase with leaf-like ornaments. In the centre of these leaves is a superb mask of Medusa, with silver eyes. The chin of the Medusa rests upon two Chimæras. Height, including base, 2 ft. 2 in.; diameter, 16½ in. (1873. *Pompeii.*)

SURROUNDING THE ROOM, AND CLOSE AGAINST THE CABINETS,

A large number of candelabra for single lamps. They are nearly all different, and many of them are very beautiful. (*Pompeii* and *Herculaneum.*)

ON THE TOP OF THE CABINETS,

Sundry kettles and amphoræ. (*Pompeii* and *H.*)

NEAR THE ENTRANCE DOOR, ON THE RIGHT,

†**Four** magnificent VASES. Observe especially the one nearest the door, the handles of which are formed by figures of gladiators. These figures are especially interesting, as they wear the spiral bronze wire anklets and gauntlets (see next room, Cabinet XXXXV.) **with** which the gladiators protected their arms and legs.

Observe next to this vase a candelabrum, with lamp fitted to slide up and down the staff. **This** specimen is unique.

CABINET No. I., TO THE **LEFT ON** ENTERING,

68747 *et seq.* Bronze baskets of very elegant form. Their folding handles are still in working order.

BELOW,

68788 *et seq.* Scoops with elegant handles, probably for taking up grain. Decorated with parrots and other birds. (*Herculaneum* and *Pompeii.*)

CABINET No. II.,

68808 *et seq.* Ten garden stools. (*Pompeii* and *H.*)

Among them,

†110673. A small SERPENT, on a miniature altar, with a gold necklace. Probably intended **for** family worship. (1875. *Pompeii.*)

68823 *et seq.* Twenty-two **small** pans, with spouts and nozzles. (*Pompeii* and *Herculaneum.*)

68843–7. Five flattened globular water-bottles, of the same shape as European soldiers use now. (*Pompeii.*)

CABINET No. III.,

*68853. PAILS (*hydriæ*). These water buckets are richly inlaid with arabesques and animals in silver and copper. Two have a double handle, which when at rest forms a rim to the pail.

On the handle of No. 68854 the words "Cornelia S. Chelidonis" are engraved. (*Pompeii* and *Herculaneum.*)

CABINET No. IV.,

68937 *et seq.* JUGS similar to those now used in Italy for oil. **From a** specimen which was found upon a trivet, and is in the next room, we learn that **these** were put on the fire. (*Pompeii* and *Herculaneum.*)

CABINET No. V.,

A large number of JUGS, with three lips and one handle, of highly artistic form. Observe Nos. 69044 to 69048. These jugs were for table use. (*Pompeii* and *Herculaneum.*)

69049. Similar JUG, with ram's head and Medusa inlaid in silver. (*Stabia.*)

BELOW,

Twelve *præfericula*, with single lip and handle. Note †69085 as being of very remarkable form. The handle is joined to the cup by the demi-bust of a woman holding fruits. A Syren issues from the edge. Unfortunately this specimen has been very much damaged. (*Pompeii.*)

69086. CUP without handles, formed in the shape of a beautiful female head, with tiara, eyes, and necklace in silver. (*Borgia.*)

†69087. LIBATION CUP, of very beautiful execution. The edge is surmounted by an eagle with its wings spread out. The handle is formed by a swan. (*Nocera.*)

OUTSIDE, ON A COLUMN UNDER GLASS,

†69089. Libation CUP, of oblong shape. This is quite a unique specimen. On the handle we observe a man and four horses plated in silver. (*Ruvo.*)

CABINET No. VI.,

Several JUGS with one handle. Observe those called " *a petto d'oca*"—that is, "*goose-breasted;*" especially

*69167. MILK-JUG, of elegant form. On its rim are two goats, showing probably that it was intended to contain milk. (*Herculaneum.*)

69168. Another JUG, of the same shape. The body of the jug is ornamented; the handle forms the perch of a parrot. (*Pompeii.*)

69169. Similar JUG, with elegant sprays in bas-relief and having a panther for its handle. (*Pompeii.*)

69171. JUG remarkable for its handle, at the bottom of which is a female mask with silver eyes, and on the top the bust of a nude female issuing from the jug, and leaning her hands on the backs of two greyhounds. (1866. *P.*)

†69174. LIBATION CUP (*rhyton*), representing the head of a stag with silver eyes. The mouth being partly open allowed the liquid to flow out. Examples of the use of this vessel will be seen in the frescoes downstairs. (*H.*)

CABINET No. VII.,

Observe Nos. 69315 to 69322.

69318. A JUG, which deserves special notice. It is ornamented with two griffins resting their claws upon an urn ; the whole is artistically chased. (*Pompeii.*)

CABINETS VIII. TO XI. (SECOND CORNER OF THE **ROOM**),

Large number of vases, which to judge by the ornaments on their handles **were** probably used for wine and other household purposes.

The handles are specially beautiful, and an endless variety of elegant form is displayed in their construction. (*Pompeii* and *Herculaneum.*)

CABINETS XII. TO XIV.,

Two-handled **ewers for** household purposes. (***Pompeii*** and *Herculaneum.*)

· *Cinerary Urns*, made of lead. (*Pompeii.*)

CABINETS XV. AND XVI. (THIRD CORNER OF THE ROOM),

FOUNTAIN JETS AND SPRAYS.

69762 *et seq.* Ten tiger heads for fountains. (*Herculaneum.*)

†69782. The head of a ram of fine workmanship, from a fountain. (*Herculaneum.*)

69784–9. A PEACOCK with spreading tail ; a column capped with three dolphins ; a pine-cone ; a serpent and a cylindrical **vase** with jet, all forming a group for a fountain.

These specimens are set up on wood to show their exact position as found. (1853. *Pompeii.*)

69791–3. Fragments of a small TANK, which was fitted with a very fine rose for producing a cascade to simulate rain. (*Pompeii.*)

69795. BASIN, with a very finely executed lion in the centre. The water flowed through his open mouth. (18th March, 1861. *Pompeii.*)

69799 *et seq.* Thirty-two taps and a lead pipe. (*P.*)

79838 *et seq.* Four GRATINGS made of perforated lead for gutters. (*Pompeii.*)

CABINET No. XVI.,

Several oblong pans. (*Pompeii.*)

In front of the window,

*73153. Curule chair (*sella curulis*), made to fold. Its four crossed legs are fastened by two nails with large heads. (*Herculaneum.*)

> In early times the honour of the *Curule chair* was due only to the kings of Rome. Subsequently, the privilege of its use was allowed to Consuls, Prætors, and Ædiles, Curules of the Republic.

First glazed table, No. XXVIII.,

One hundred and forty-three vase handles, finely executed and adorned with heads and arabesques.

72578 to 72581. These four are in the style known as " *a voluta.*" They are cunningly entwined and finish into small acanthus leaves.

72582–3. Two serpentine handles, each serpent holding a cockchafer in his mouth.

72591. Handle representing in bas-relief a cross-legged Faun, playing the pan-pipe; and above, the bust of a woman with her hands on the necks of two dogs.

†72592. Very fine handle, representing a Phrygian with a pair of shoes on, and his feet crossed. He stands on the mask of a bearded man. (*Pompeii.*)

72594. Handle. The point of contact with the vase represents in bas-relief a woman extracting a thorn from the right foot of a man. (*Borgia.*)

†72600. Superb Handle, the gem of the collection, adorned with arabesques and inlaid in silver, with a head of Medusa of exquisite finish. (*Herculaneum.*)

72637. Fine Handle. The point of contact with the vase represents the bust of Apollo holding the lyre and the *plectrum*. Below, a swan with spreading wings. (*P.*)

Next table, No. XXIX.,

72722–3. Two legs of a table, with lions' claws, each representing an armless Sphinx issuing from three leaves. (*Pompeii.*)

72727 *et seq.* Four legs of a table, with greyhound claws. (*Pompeii.*)

Cabinet No. XVII.,

BATHING REQUISITES.

*Strigils (*strigilis*), used by the ancients after gymnastic exercises and vapour baths to scrape off the perspiration and the ointments. (*Pompeii* and *Herculaneum.*)

*69962-3. On an antique ring are strung two strigils (the best in the collection), the handles representing busts of Diana and Hercules. (*Pompeii.*)

69904. Complete apparatus for Roman bath, consisting of an opening ring upon which are strung four strigils, one *patera* or shallow **saucer** with handle for mixing the ointments in, and one ointment pot. (*Pompeii.*)

Sundry small pots (*guttus* or *unguentarium*) in bronze or alabaster, for containing perfumed ointments. (*P. and H.*)

> Pliny tells us that the alabaster pots were preferable, and we may infer that they were used for the more costly ointments. These were hermetically sealed, and the expression "she brake the box" (Mark **xiv.** 3) may probably mean "she brake open the box."

Cylindrical vase in ivory, covered with Bacchanalian figures. (*Asia Minor.*)

BELOW,

Ornamental bronze **claws** for furniture. Sundry strigils.

70127 *et seq.* Several small pans, thought by some to **have** been used for horseshoes. In our opinion this could **not** have been the case, as the nailholes are seen to be all **round** them, which would involve driving the nails into the frog of the foot. Besides, the reverse is decorated with a bas-relief. Undoubted specimens **of** horseshoes of this period may be seen in the British **Museum.** (*P. and H.*)

CABINETS XVIII. TO XX.,

LOCKS AND KEYS.

70981 *et seq.* Long borders inlaid with silver, serving as horizontals for bedsteads. (*Pompeii.*)

LOCKS in bronze and iron. Some have keys belonging to them. (*P. and H.*)

Sundry keys of all sizes, some of which are very complicated. (*P. and H.*)

†71401. Iron KEY, carefully made and inlaid with silver. It was found upon one of the **skeletons** of the family of *Diomede*, in the cellar of his house at Pompeii.

71392 *et seq.* Bolts of locks. (*Pompeii.*)

71465. Iron skeleton key. (*Pompeii.*)

Sundry hinges. (*Pompeii* and *Herculaneum.*)

BELOW,

71629 and 71630. Two large hinges from one of the

city gates of Pompeii. Similar hinges were some years ago shown to a celebrated Neapolitan antiquary (as a new invention) at Woolwich Arsenal, to his great amusement.

GLAZED TABLE, No. XXX.,

Ornaments for doors and furniture, including tragic and comic masks and busts; heads of lions, horses, and other animals, with movable rings passed through their mouths. (*Pompeii* and *Herculaneum*.)

†7282–2 and –4. Rectangular panels, on which are bas-reliefs of a Centaur playing the lyre and a female Centaur playing the double flute. Very fine. (*Pompeii*.)

72823. VENUS seated by Bacchus, accompanied by Silenus. A fine bas-relief, intended for a safe. (*Pompeii*.)

GLAZED TABLE, No. XXXI.,

72898 *et seq.* HANDLES for vases, formed of two dolphins. (*Pompeii*.)

Other handles ending in foliage and human hands. (*Pompeii* and *Herculaneum*.)

STATUETTES serving as handles for vases.

†72960. A female figure of wonderful expression, resting her feet on a serpent and supporting on her head an architrave to which the vase was fitted.

72963. KNOCKER of a door, representing in *alto-rilievo* the bust of Diana armed with a quiver. (*Pompeii*.)

†72966–7. Four KNOCKERS with movable rings. These represent in bas-relief superb heads of Medusa with silver eyes, and the two larger ones with silver teeth. (1870. *Pompeii*.)

The work of these specimens, and especially of the two centre ones, is exquisite. Alone, they prove the high perfection of ancient art.

72970. Door knocker (ring lost), representing in bas-relief the head of a woman, with fine expression and mouth partly open. (*Pompeii*.)

72972. Pretty furniture ornament, representing a Cupid seated between the tails of two sea-horses. (*Herculaneum*.)

†72981. Large HANDLE for furniture, with winged Genii in bas-relief, having their heads pillowed on their entwined arms, and (on the sides) two Tritons with cuirasses in a striking attitude. This specimen is in the Etruscan style. Duplicate in the British Museum. (*Borgia*.)

In front of the window,

†73152. Curule chair (*sella curulis*), made to fold, with remains of gilding still discernible. It was originally mounted in ivory, which has been replaced by wood. (*P.*)

(The original ivory is exhibited in fragments in the next room, Glazed Table LXVII.)

Cabinet XXI. (last corner of the room),

IRON TOOLS.

. 71700 *et seq.* Scythes, sickles, bill-hooks, knives. (*P.* and *H.*)

71733 *et seq.* Rakes and forks with two and three teeth, four ploughshares, spades as used in Naples now, and trowels for gardening. (*P.* and *H.*)

Cabinet No. **XXII.,**

Carding combs, long shovel, large spring shears; **shears** of this form still used in silk factories. (1877. *Pompeii.*)

Sundry smaller shears, blacksmiths' cutters and pincers, axes and hatchets (*securis, ascia*); soldering iron, claws for drawing nails, pickaxes, wedges, and hammers for chipping pavements. (*P.* and *H.*)

Cabinet No. **XXIII.**

Hammers for carpenters and masons. (*Pompeii.*)

†71875. Key for raising heavy blocks of stone (as used now), compasses, callipers, masons' trowels, turnery tools, centre-bits, scalpels, planes, saws, anvils, a large whetstone.

Cabinet No. XXIV.,

LAMPS AND LANTERNS.

· **72067.** Lantern glazed with talc, bearing on the top **the** words "Tiburti Catus S." This lantern was found near the skeletons in the cellar of the House of Diomede at Pompeii.

72166. **Dou**ble-wick lamp, **bearing** inscription " D. Iuni Proquli." (*Pompeii.*)

72172. Single lamp, adapted either to hang or carry, fitted with a chain to which the lid is attached. A small mouse on the spout is about to gnaw the wick. (*Pompeii.*)

The mouse was sacred to Vulcan, and perhaps this lamp hung before his shrine.

†72180. Magnificent treble-wick lamp, fitted with three exquisite double-stranded chains to hang it by; a fourth chain holds the lid of the reservoir. This lamp is adorned with four heads issuing from garlands. (*Pompeii.*)

72181. Large treble-wick LAMP. Instead of a cover it has a handsome urn over the reservoir which contains the oil. This lamp is unique in point of form, and is adorned with festoons and three masks. (*Pompeii.*)

72187. Single LAMP. A horse's head upon the handle. The original wick is visible. (*Pompeii.*)

Sundry CANDELABRA for single lamps. (*P.* and *H.*)

CABINET No. XXV.,

72190. CANDELABRUM in the form of a cvp. (*P.*)

72191. CANDELABRUM formed of a fluted column, with four boughs to carry hanging lamps. (*H.*)

72192–3. Two pretty CANDELABRA (like modern candlesticks), the top representing a lotus-flower. (*Pompeii.*)

72195. CANDELABRUM formed of a fluted column capped by a small vase, from which issue three branches. (*P.*) Upon the plinth an octagonal pedestal, upon which is a globe. This plinth is inlaid with silver. (*Pompeii.*)

72246 and 72250. Treble-wick lamps with *elychnium*, hanging by a well-wrought chain, and decorated with a nude dancer.

72251. Double lamps with garland and sunflower handle. The cover represents a child with a goose.

CABINET No. XXVI.,

72198. Treble-wick circular LAMP. The lid, which also forms a handle, is surmounted by the figure of a Harpy, in Etruscan style. (*Pompeii.*)

72199. Drunken SILENUS. His movement and the gestures of his hands lead us to infer that he proposes to dance. (*Nemo saltat sobrius.*) Behind him, a parrot on a bough which carries two lamps. (*Pompeii.*)

72202–3. PHRYGIAN figure on one knee. Behind him, the stump of a tree with a lamp upon it. (*Pompeii.*)

†72206. LAMP-STAND. Drunken Silenus, seated on a rock, pouring wine from a wineskin which he holds in his left hand. Behind him, a stump to carry two lamps. (*Pompeii.*)

72209. LAMP-STAND. Silenus with a basket on his head. Behind him, a stump bearing a cup to carry a lamp. (August 17, 1876. *Pompeii.*)

72279. DOUBLE-WICK LAMP (*dimyxos*). The handle is ornamented with an acanthus. The lid represents a

Satyr seated on a stump, holding a pan-pipe in his left hand ; one of the original wicks is in its place. (Feb. 21, 1868. *Pompeii.*)

72280. Fine LAMP, with two wicks adorned with beautiful sprays. The lid bears a Silenus standing upright. (*Pompeii.*)

†72291. Handsome small CANDELABRUM, fitted to be carried or hung by the chains attached to it. It represents Cupid astride on a dolphin, which is about to devour a polypus issuing from a shell. A wonderful work of art, for the harmony of the grouping and the expression of the Cupid, who betrays alarm at what is passing beneath him. (*House of Marcus Lucretius, Pompeii.*)

110674. Single LAMP, representing a goose with movable neck. (*Pompeii.*)

72292. Small SILENUS, holding a bowl which could be used as a lamp. The pose of this figure is admirable. (*P.*)

†72298. NIGHT-LIGHT in a saucer. The lid is perforated to subdue the light. (*Stabia.*)

CABINET No. XXVII.,

72226. CANDELABRUM in the form of the trunk of a tree. From the boughs are suspended three lamps, of which two are in the shape of snails. (June 13, 1772. *Pompeii.*)

72231. CANDELABRUM in the form of a tree, the boughs supporting five double-wick lamps. (*Herculaneum.*)

72333. Bronze FISH, perhaps a dolphin, constructed as a lamp. The wick passed through the creature's mouth. On the back, the feet of a statuette which is lost. (*P.*)

†72336. Portable lamp with one wick and long folding handle. (*Stabia.*)

END OF FIRST ROOM.

SECOND ROOM.

In the centre of this room stands a cork model of the excavations of Pompeii, on the scale of 1 to 100. It is extremely accurate, and well worthy of attention, as giving a bird's-eye view of the city, such as can be obtained in no other situation.

The wooden balustrade shows the perimeter of the city,

and represents the outline of the ancient ramparts, while the part painted green shows what yet remains to be excavated.

The amphitheatre, which was capable of holding 12,800 people, was situated either at one of the extremities of the town as shown on the model, or perhaps without the walls.

The extent of the city is estimated at about one hundred and forty acres, and the part excavated may be taken at about fifty acres, leaving ninety acres still buried beneath a mass of volcanic ash about twenty feet deep, which has been cultivated and even built upon for centuries. The length of the excavated portion is about six hundred yards, and the circuit of the city two miles.

If the visitor stands opposite to the windows of the room at the left end of the model, he will have the Porta Marina of Pompeii, by which we now enter the ruins, opposite to him. Entering by that gate, he sees the *Basilica* or Law Court on his right hand, the Temple of Venus opposite on his left—both touching the large open space which was the ancient Forum, and which had (in common with all the public buildings) a colonnade running round it. At the further end of the Forum was the Temple of Jupiter, and beyond it on the right that of Fortune, and, on the left, one of the public baths, easily distinguished by its dome and roofs, which are still standing. Returning to the Forum, we see on the right the Pantheon, recognised by the pedestals of the statues, which stand in a group in the court. Next to that, the *Curia Senatorum* or "Town Hall." Then the Temple of Mercury, and, adjoining this, the Exchange, where the statue of Eumachia which was erected by the Fullers can be recognised in the model.

Leaving the Forum by the broad "Street of Abundance," which runs right across the city, we come to the principal public baths, and on the extreme right of the spectator the Temple of Isis, the two theatres, the triangular Forum, and the barracks (*ludi Gladiatorii*).

The gate leading to the "Street of the Tombs" is on the spectator's left, and at the point nearest to the window. The House of Diomede and the Street of the Tombs being outside the walls, are not represented on the model.

c

AGAINST THE BALUSTRADE OF **THE** MODEL,

Twelve circular leaden tanks for the *impluvia* of houses, found in the courtyards. They **were** lime-washed to purify the rain-water. One of them has a bronze tap. (*P.*)

SAUCEPANS, PATERÆ, &c.

ON THE LEFT, CABINETS XXXII. AND XXXIII.,

SAUCEPANS, of which many are lined with silver; some bear their maker's name.

7233. A saucepan as found at Herculaneum, completely full of lava and encrusted with ash.

CABINETS XXXIV. AND XXXV.,

Sundry PATERÆ (or bowls for containing libations). They **are** of the shape of a deep saucer, with a handle ending generally in the head of a ram or a swan. Observe Nos. 73439, 73440, 73455, and 73484. These are handsomely worked and inlaid with **silver.** (*Pompeii* and *Herculaneum.*)

CABINET XXXVI. (*among a number of two-handled basins*),

73511. BAS-RELIEF in silver of Æthra showing her son Theseus **the** sword that his father Ægeus had hidden under a rock. (*Herculaneum.*)

> Ægeus, king of Athens, promised to acknowledge his son Theseus as soon as he could lift this rock and bear away the sword. This he did, and came to Athens, to find his father living with Medea, who forthwith attempted to poison him. His father having identified him by the sword, sent him to Crete to slay the Minotaur, and on his return he forgot to hoist white sails as arranged; and Ægeus, seeing black sails, threw himself into the sea, which was called Ægean after him.

CABINET XXXVII.,

73535. BASIN. Two figures in bas-relief, one dancing. (*Herculaneum.*)

73549. BASIN on a tripod with ornate border. The handles are lions, and **the sides bear four** serpents. (*P.*)

CABINET XXXVIV.,

73613. BASIN with a bas-relief of a woman fashioning a trophy, and Hercules with his club standing by. (*H.*)

CABINET XXXXIV.,

LADLES (*cyathus* and *simpulum*) used for dipping into vases. (*Pompeii* and *Herculaneum.*)

CABINET XXXXV. (SECOND CORNER OF THE ROOM),

73838–73863. Twenty-six funnels. (*P.* and *H.*)

73879-80-81. Three round stoves. The first has a lid whose handle is formed by a statuette of a slave seated, with his hands tied behind him; between them he holds a ring, fastened to a bronze chain. (*Pompeii.*)

*73882. URN (*authepsa*), with two handles and lions' feet. Inside, a vertical cylinder for live charcoal, with perforations below for draught. Round this cylinder lay the hot spiced wine (*calida*), which was drawn off by a tap in the front, placed high up to prevent the sediment choking it. On the right, a cup or conduit by which the vessel might be filled without taking off the lid. Inside was a false lid, which closed the whole urn except the mouth of the furnace, thus preventing the ash from polluting the liquid.

This beautiful urn is decorated with designs, and is similar to the Russian *Samovar* and the old-fashioned English tea-urn. (*Pompeii.*)

111048. Another elegant URN, found February 8, 1876. It stands on three lions' feet, and is ornamented with three female masks. The tap represents Cupid astride on a dolphin. (*Pompeii.*)

BELOW,

73886 *et seq.* FEET for vases. (*P.* and *H.*)

73937. Bronze RING for slaves, bearing the inscription: "Servus sum, tene quia fugio" (*I am a slave; hold me lest I escape*).

73940. Large SERPENT in gilt bronze. Possibly the arm of a chair. (*Borgia.*)

73934. MANACLES for slaves.

SPIRAL GAUNTLETS in bronze, which gladiators wore as a protection for their arms and legs.

BONES of a child, round which a long bronze wire is twisted. (*Found in a tomb at Sant' Angelo, near Capua.*)

CABINET XXXXVI.,

ARTICLES USED IN SACRIFICES.

73945 *et seq.* Four portable ALTARS on three legs, supporting a disc which received the blood of victims. (*Pompeii.*)

†74021-2-3. FLESH-HOOKS (*harpago*) for taking boiled meat out of the caldron (see Exodus xxvii. 3, 1 Sam. ii.

13, 14; Aristoph. Vesp. 1152). They were fitted with wooden handles. There are four similar specimens in the British Museum. (*Canino.*)

73996 *et seq.* Small ALTARS for incense. Very fine. (*Pompeii* and *Herculaneum.*)

73983 *et seq.* Censers (*turibula*), with chains and spoons for incense, not to be confounded with the Jewish censer, which seems, like the modern ones, to have been portable and waved in the air. (*Pompeii* and *Herculaneum.*)

74002. Handle of SPRINKLER, for scattering lustral water. Found in the laver in the Temple of Isis. The hair is modern, but restored from a bas-relief found at Rome. (*P.*)

74003 *et seq. Mensæ* for the Augurs (*aruspica*). They are in the shape of a stool. Upon them lie the instruments (*lingulæ*) which were used to examine the entrails of the victims for the **purposes** of pretended **prophecy.** (*P.*)

BELOW,

Bronze letters for shop-fronts. (*Pompeii.*)

BEDSTEADS.

†78614. Three BEDSTEADS. Two have heads to them. The wooden part painted **red is a restoration**; the original wood **was** walnut.

The obverse of these bedsteads **is** richly inlaid with silver and decorated with a *genius* **in** relief holding a rabbit, which he is feeding with grapes (much injured). **On** the reverse **is** a goose's head. Height, **18** in.; head, 20¼ in.; length, 7 ft. 7 in.; width, 4 ft. (*Pompeii.*)

Notice the old-fashioned "*trundle-bed*" beneath the centre bedstead. Found in 1868, in the house of Vibius at Pompeii.

In the garden of this house is a well twenty-five metres in
depth, which still contains water. This water corresponds
exactly to the height of Pompeii above the sea-level.

78613. Small round table. The three legs represent greyhounds jumping up. (*Pompeii.*)

UPON THIS TABLE IS PLACED,

†78673. Two-handled ewer of **very** remarkable construction, supported on three Sphinxes with lions' claws, and intended for heating water. The fire lay on a grating of hollow tubes at the bottom. The water circulated through these tubes, and was heated in the jacket, which

surrounded the coals in the centre of the vase, exactly on the principle of modern tubular boilers. (*Pompeii.*)

WEIGHTS AND MEASURES.

Cabinet XXXXVII.,

Eighteen STEELYARDS and SCALES, complete.

All the scale-pans are ornamented and held up by chains of beautiful workmanship. A sliding ring upon the chains secured the goods in the pan while they were being weighed. The sliding weight on the beam of the steelyards represents the reigning Emperor. The beams are graduated with numbers, from I. to XIII. and a half on the obverse, and from X. to XXXX. on the reverse, to weigh heavier goods.

74039. The sixth scale from the visitor's left bears the inscription (in dotted lines): "TI. CLAUD. CÆS. ÆIIII. VITEL. III. COS. EXACTA. III. TIC. CURA. AEDIL.;" meaning that this balance was stamped at the Capitol in the reign of the Emperor Claudius. The sliding weight represents this Emperor. (*Pompeii.*)

Cabinet IL.,

·†74056. Under the hook from which this specimen hangs we read the inscription, "IMP. VESP. AUG. IIX. T. IMP. AUG. F. VI. COS. EXACTA. IN CAPITO(*lio*);" that is to say, that it was stamped in the Capitol under the eighth consulate of the Emperor Vespasian, and under the sixth of Titus, which corresponds to A.D. 77, two years only before the destruction of Pompeii. The weight represents the bust of Vespasian. (*Pompeii.*)

74062. Steelyards fitted with hooks instead of pans, to hold the goods to be weighed. (*Pompeii.*)

74084. Very small scales. In the place of one of the pans is a coin of the Emperor Augustus. (*Pompeii.*)

74165. Ingenious machine for weighing liquids. It is in the form of a saucepan, and was suspended by the hook and chain. The liquid to be weighed was then put in the pan, and the equilibrium was adjusted by means of weights fastened to the ring beneath, and by shifting the position of the hook-chain along the graduated slot, which bears the symbols: | ··· | ··· | ·· | IV : ≡≡≡ | · | ·XI· | ·XI· | (*Pompeii.*)

Sundry round weights in black basalt (*nefritica*), marked in Roman figures.

We subjoin a table of these weights.

ROUND WEIGHTS IN BLACK STONE (*nefritica*).

74179. Weight marked XX, equal to kilos. 6,460,40
74180.   „   „   X,   „   „   3,404,10
74181.   „   „.   X,   „   „   3,249,60

This last bears the inscription : L. ATILIUS FIILIX MAG. MAR D. S. D.

74182. Weight marked X, equal to kilos. 3,232,30
74183.   „   „   X,   „   „   3,226,70
74184.   „   „   X,   „   „   3,224,00
74185.   „   „   X,   „   „   3,223,25
74186.   „   „   X,   „   „   3,222,70
74187.   „   „   X,   „   „   3,123,60
74188.   „   „   „   „   3,290,90
74189.   „   „   V,   „   „   1,619,35
74190.   „   „   V,   „   „   1,616,55
74191.   „   „   V,   „   „   1,616,20
74192.   „   „   V,   „   „   1,612,00
74193.   „   „   V,   „   „   1,608,70
74194.   „   „   „   „   1,605,40
74195.   „   „   „   „   1,590,70
74196.   „   „   V,   „   „   1,414,50

74213. This weight bears the inscription : EX - AUC-TO(*ritate*) IUNI RUSTICI.

74280 to 74290. Eleven round weights in bronze, marked with silver numerals, X, V, III, II, I, S or "*semis*" (half), for the pounds, and :: ⋰ : . S for fractions of pounds.

GLANDULAR BRONZE WEIGHTS.

74295. Weight marked V, equal to kilos. 1,668,50
74296.   „   „   „   „   1,653,70
74297.   „   „   III,   „   „   1,031,50
74298.   „   „   II,   „   „   0,658,60
74299.   „   „   „   „   0,339,40
74300.   „   — S (*semis*)   „   „   0,153,45
74301.   „   — ⋰   „   „   0,088,65
74302.   „   — :   „   „   0,084,20
74303.   „   — .   „   „   0,034,10

74307. Bronze WEIGHT, in the shape of a fish. Equal to kilos. 0·63780.

74308 to 74313. **Six** bronze WEIGHTS, in the shape **of** goats, probably used for weighing goats' meat. These are marked P.X, P.V, P.III, P.II, P.I.

The last but one bears the inscription, STALLI FELIC. (Oct. 14th, 1863. *Pompeii*.)

Nest of bronze weights, in the shape of mortars. The largest answers to the *decempondium*, and is equal to kilos. 3·04380.

74315. Equal to kilos.		1,631,40
74316.	„	„ 0,984,40
74317.	„	„ 0,162,20
74318.	„	„ 0,108,00
74319.	„	„ 0,081,35
74320.	„	„ 0,054,20

74390 to 74393. **Four** large weights, bearing the shape of the meat they were used for; a PIG, bearing the initials P.C (one hundred pounds); a CHEESE, and two huge KNUCKLE-BONES. (*Pompeii*.)

Smaller leaden weights, bearing the word "EME" on one side and "HABEBIS" on the other—"*Buy, and you shall have.*"

74582 *et seq.* Measures for oil. They bear an olive on the handles. (*Pompeii*.)

74599. Measure for liquids,—the *congius* spoken of by Pliny. A long-necked vase without handle, bearing the inscription: IMP. CAESARE VESPAS. VI. T. CAES. AUG. F. IIII COS. MENSURAE EXACTAE IN CAPITOLIO P. X.—"measure of the weight of ten pounds, gauged at the Capitol in the sixth consulate of the Emperor Cæsar Vespasian and the fourth of his son Titus Augustus Cæsar." (*Borgia*.)

74600–1. MEASURES for dry goods. Their capacity was settled by the triangular crosspieces. Inscription: "D. D. P. P. HERC." (*Pompeii*.)

OUTSIDE THE CABINET,

74602. Dry measure. (The wood is a restoration.) (*P*.)

CABINETS L. AND LI.,

Sundry kitchen utensils. (*Pompeii* and *Herculaneum*.)

SCULPTOR'S INSTRUMENTS.

GLAZED TABLE LXI.,

76657 to 76667. Plummets. (*P*. and *H*.)

76670 *et seq.* Sundry pairs of compasses. (*P*. and *H*.)

76684. Reducing compasses. (*Pompeii.*)
76690 *et seq.* Linear measures. (*P.*)
76689. Square. (*P.*)

FISHING TACKLE.

Netting needles, bronze and bone needles, quadruple fish-hook weighted, four hundred and forty common fish-hooks.

109703. A RUDDER, belonging probably to a bronze statue of "Abundance," who was usually represented with one. (*P.*)

Small anchor; the only one yet found. Gift of Baron Savarese. (1882. *P.*)

MUSICAL INSTRUMENTS.

GLAZED TABLE No. LXII.,

76945 *et seq.* Systra—jingling bronze rattles used in the worship of Isis, and still to be found among the natives of Nubia. These are decorated with a representation of Romulus and Remus sucking the wolf. (*P.*)

76942. Cymbals of two kinds. (*Pompeii.*)

11055. A bronze wind instrument, like an organ. No certain explanation can be given of this fragment. It was fitted with a chain, apparently to be carried round the neck. (1876. *Pompeii.*)

76887. Tibia or flageolet. (*P.*)

*76890. Bagpipes found in the barracks. The "dulcimer" of Dan. iii. 5. (*Pompeii.*)

76891 *et seq.* Four single FLAGEOLETS, made of silver, bronze, and ivory. (1869. *P.*)

> The modern flageolet lying by them was made of the same materials as an experiment, in imitation of the ancient ones, and has been much approved for its tone by musical critics both here and in Germany.

TOYS—DICE AND TICKETS FOR THEATRES.

GLAZED TABLE LXIII.,

†Knucklebones and dice; some constructed that they might be loaded. (*Pompeii.*)

Nine conical specimens in carbonised wood, supposed to be children's tops. (*Pompeii* and *Herculaneum.*)

†77087 *et seq.* Sundry checks or tickets (*tesseræ*) for theatres and boxing matches, made of ivory. Some bear

the names of the play, some the number of the seat, others names, as "Æschylus," " Arpax," " Vapio," " Pernix,"&c. Observe the small numbered pigeons made of terra-cotta. These were checks for the upper row of seats, still called the *"piccionaia,"* or pigeon-loft, at Naples. (*P.* and *H.*)

'. The above is the received explanation, but we cannot vouch for it.

1990880. Six death's-heads (use unknown), numbered II, III, IV, VIII, IX, X. Found 21st Sept., 1873. (*Pompeii.*)

77076. Earthenware DEATH'S-HEAD, bearing the inscription " ΗΔΥΛΟϹ " and the number VI. (*Herculaneum.*)

TOILET REQUISITES.

GLAZED TABLE LXIII. (*bis*),

77146. Small bit of chain, to which is attached a crystal tassel for a trinket. (*P.*)

77147 *et seq.* Bronze clasps (*fibulae*), one in the form of a horse. (*P.* and *H.*)

77259 *et seq.* Bronze rings fitted with a small key for jewel cases. (*Pompeii.*)

77269. Very large ring, for use as a seal, or possibly it belonged to a statue. (*P.*) Sundry rings in bone and lead, bearing initials and numbers. (*P.*)

77174 *et seq.* Bronze bracelets, in the form of serpents, one with a silver medallion. (1863. *P.*)

77184. Ten bone beads, part of a necklace; hairpins in bronze, in form of a serpent; a caduceus; Venus dressing. One of these, representing Venus and Cupid, stood in a glass jar, which we now see twisted up all round it by the heat. (*P.*)

77213 *et seq.* Five perfect metal MIRRORS. One in a modern frame was found in the House of the Faun. (*P.*)

77291 *et seq.* These specimens have hitherto been supposed to be perforated boxes for perfumes, made on the principle of the modern " *vinaigrette ;* " but in our opinion they are cases for seals to be attached to parchments. The box would contain the seal, and two or more threads of silk attached to the wax would pass from the parchment through the holes and be attached by the wax and the impression, while the case would preserve the seal intact. One of them may be seen represented upon the large fresco from the House of Pansa attached to the papyrus.

77298. Small rectangular bolts in ivory, for securing dressing cases or small articles of furniture. (P.)

Bone buttons and bronze studs. (P.)

77355 *et seq.* Ivory and bronze combs. (*Pompeii.*)

77363. BRONZE THIMBLE. This specimen is very large, and must probably **have** been intended for a man. Perhaps it was used upon the thumb, as it used to be in England, where its original name **was** "*thumble.*" (P.)

Sundry small pots for cosmetics.

77569. Small ivory pot, adorned with a pretty bas-relief of Cupids, one playing the flageolet. (*Pompeii.*)

77570. Pot of rock-crystal, still containing *rouge.* (2 Kings ix. 30.) (*Pompeii.*)

Sundry small flagons in alabaster and **ivory,** for perfumes. (P.)

SPINDLE, fitted **with a bronze hook.** (P.)

> Possi**bly the** point was originally straight, and the implement **was an** ordinary spindle. The upper part of it favours this **idea.** At any rate the specimen is unique.

77518. Bronze **winder, in** nine divisions, for threads of different colours. (**P.**)

77544–5. Two needle-cases (?). (**P.**)

A small alabaster bowl containing pins.

8088. Small toothed wheel, used as part of a bolt. (P.)

> We draw attention to this little specimen, to show how nearly the Romans had reached one of the leading principles of the modern clock.

Hairpins in bone, adorned **with** statuettes and busts; **toothpicks** and earpickers. (*P.* and *H.*)

> **As to** the antiquity of such ornaments, see Isaiah iii. 18.

CABINETS LII. AND LIII., AGAINST THE WALL,

Kitchen pots and pans. (*P.* and *H.*)

COLANDERS.

CASE LXIV., IN FRONT OF THE WINDOW,

Colanders perforated in graceful designs. (*P.* and *H.*)

77609. In the centre of this specimen a bas-relief of

Venus with silver bracelets, holding out her hand to a small Cupid. (*Herculaneum.*)

These colanders are so elegant, that they must probably have been intended for table use. The received theory is, that they were filled with snow and dipped into the wine-bowls, and served to keep the impurities from the snow out of the wine.

Near the balustrade of the model of Pompeii,

78579. Large CALDRON, nailed and bolted as our modern steam boilers. (*Pompeii.*)

78580. Large fire-plug, found in the palace of Tiberius at Capri. The rust of ages has sealed it hermetically. Till within two years this specimen had some water in it, which one could hear by shaking it. This water appears now to have completely evaporated. Height, 1 ft. 9 in.; length, 2 ft. 5 in.; diameter of pipe, 7 in.

78581. Bronze grating (*claustrum*), found before a window in Pompeii.

GLAZED TABLES LXV. AND LXVI. (THE SECOND CONTAINS THE MORE IMPORTANT SPECIMENS),

SURGICAL INSTRUMENTS (*Chirurgia*).

We have been favoured with the following description of these instruments by Dr. Barringer of Naples. Most of them were found in the "*House of the Surgeon*" at Pompeii, and differ but little from those in use at the present day.

GLAZED TABLE LXV.,

Bistouries (surgical knives), spatulæ, sounds, and pincers, some of which last belonged to lamps.

77738 *et seq.* "Directors."

77982. Curved dentated forceps, for removing foreign substances from cavities. The curved extremity of the branches is hollowed out, and the teeth fit into each other.

77985. Digitated forceps bearing the name "*Acaecolus.*" These are used for holding open the lips of a wound while a deeper incision is being made. They are usually made now with curved ends and small teeth.

GLAZED TABLE LXVI.,

77986 *et seq.* Fourteen bronze cupping vessels of modern shape, but ours are now made of glass.

78000-1. Spoons ending in the head of a ram and of a woman.

78003. Lancet for bleeding.

78004. Silver spoon with elegant handle.

78005. Scissors with a spring, like shears.

78007. FLEAM for bleeding horses.

78008. TROCHAR for tapping for dropsy. A hole in the end gives an exit to the water.

78012. An ELEVATOR (or instrument for raising depressed portions of the skull) made of bronze, five inches long, and very much resembling those made **use** of in the present day.

78026. A MALE CATHETER (*ænea fistula*), **ten** inches in length. The shape is remarkable, from **its** having the double curve like the letter S, which is the **form** that was re-invented in the last century by the celebrated French surgeon, J. L. Petit. It is open at one end, closed at the other. At the closed end is an eye, as in the modern instrument.

78027. A FEMALE CATHETER, $3\frac{1}{2}$ inches in length. (See Celsus, **de** Med. vii. 26, § 1, p. 429.)

78029. POMPEIAN FORCEPS, formed of two branches crossing, and working on a pivot. Each branch is fitted with **an** engine-turned handle and a spoon-shaped blade. The length of the handles gives great power to the operator, and the curve of the blades enables the surgeon to see what he is doing. The blades are fluted on their contiguous surfaces, and these grooves fit exactly into one another, thus affording a firm hold even when an operation requires considerable force. It was used for crushing small *calculi*. Length, 8 inches.

*78030. SPECULUM UTERI. Professional men have **dis**cussed this instrument very closely. (See the works of Vulpes and Quaranta.) It is a tri-valvular speculum: the three valves, standing at right angles to the rest of the instrument, are jointly dependent on each other in the expansion transmitted only to one of them.

When the three valves are in contact, the instrument for insertion is about an inch in circumference. By turning the screw, one valve is drawn nearer to the operator, and this forces the other two to open in a side-long direction, producing thus a slow, regular, progressive dilatation, as extensive as may be required. The instrument can be held by the two curved handles in the left hand, while the right hand turns the screw. These movable handles are similar to those fitted to modern specula. Length, 8¼ inches; widest expansion of valves, 1½ inches.

78031. SPECULUM ANI. A bi-valvular speculum, probably used also for the uterus before the other one was known. This instrument is opened or closed by means of the pivot in the centre. It has been the model of modern specula.

78032. Dentated forceps, of elegant construction, with hollowed blades.

78121. Sound, with flattened extremity, bifurcated for cutting the frenum of the tongue; as used in modern surgery.

78034 et seq. Actual cauteries.

78071. Surgical needle.

78037. Probes found in the cases to the left of them. Some are inlaid with silver, and all are perfectly preserved.

78195–6. Stones for sharpening instruments.

78037 et seq. Sundry hooks and instrument cases.

78197. Case of SURGICAL INSTRUMENTS. It is fitted to a slab of basanite, used to mix medicines on.

78235. An INJECTION PROBE for females, with eight small holes arranged like wreaths, as in the best modern instruments, thus insuring a separate and gentle flow.

The other end is obviously shaped to be fitted with a syringe.

Sundry boxes containing PILLS, SULPHUR, and other medicaments.

IVORY ARTICLES.

LAST GLAZED TABLE LXVII.,

Lions' claws for furniture; bosses and other fragments of the Curule chair in the first room. (P.)

Medallions and statuettes for furniture.

110924. Statuette of Venus with a dolphin. (Pompeii.)

78279. Statuette of a boy wearing the bulla patritia, the badge of patrician birth (see p. 33). (Pompeii.)

109905 and –5 bis. Two ivory PANELS (frame modern), carved on both sides, adapted as ornaments for furniture.

The one (No. 109905) represents, on the side that one cannot see, a wounded hero carried by two attendants. The exposed side is a continuation of the episode : the same hero is seated near a tree ; a woman kneeling by him is dressing his wound ; behind him stands an attendant.

The other panel (No. 109905 *bis*), which no doubt belonged to the same article of furniture, represents Pluto capturing Proserpine in a *quadriga* on the one side, and on the other Minerva, Diana, and Ceres. (April 1873. *P.*)

78289. Fine ivory death's-head. (*Pompeii.*)

78288. Small **bronze skeleton.** (*Pompeii.*)

78445. Bone spoons. (*Pompeii.*)

WRITING MATERIALS.
CABINET LVI.,

Sundry inkstands, pens, metal mirrors, *porte-bonheur* bracelets. (*Pompeii.*)

75080. Inkstand (*atramentum*), still containing ink.

†75091. Octagonal inkstand (found in a tomb at Terlizzi) of bronze, decorated in silver, with the seven divinities who presided over the seven days of the week, —namely, Apollo, Diana, Mars, Mercury, Jupiter, Venus, and **Saturn.**

Martorelli, the archæologist (who wrote two volumes about this inkstand), thinks that it **belonged to** some astronomer of the time of Trajan.

110672. Bronze PEN, nibbed like a modern one. (*P.*)

IN A TUBE OF MODERN GLASS,

75095. Another pen of reed, found in a papyrus **at** Herculaneum.

70099. **Slabs of** stone, which were covered with wax for writing upon with the "*stylus.*"

75113. Two bone "*styli.*" Pointed at one end and flat **at the other,** to correct **or rub out** what one had written. (*Pompeii.*)

BELOW,

80111. BRACELET on the bone of a human arm. (*P.*)

Sundry small BONE TUBES. The large charred fragment in this case, found in Herculaneum, shows us that these tubes were used for hinges. (*P.*)

SADDLERY.

CABINET (NEXT THE DOOR) LVII.,

CATTLE BELLS, HARNESS, &c. Large number of bells for cattle. By pulling a wire in the side of this case, one of these bells is made to ring. (*Pompeii* and *Herculaneum.*)

75478. Small model of a BIGA, of very great interest, as showing us the form of Pompeian vehicles.

75479–75480. Small model waggon and *biga.* (*Borgia.*)

HARNESS FOR HORSES (*ephippium*), consisting of scrolls, sprays, bits, nosebands, poleheads, curb-chains, spurs, stirrups (?), buckles, and other objects which can be readily identified.

75537. HOOF-PARER (?). The blade is gone, but the handle represents a blacksmith in the act of paring a hoof.

KITCHEN UTENSILS.

CABINET LVIII.,

PASTRY MOULDS in the shape of shells. (*P.* and *H.*)

76352 *et seq.* Four SHAPES, representing a hare, a pig, a ham, and half a fowl. (*Pompeii.*)

76336. IMPLEMENTS for making pastry. Pastry cutters.

76349. Cheese-graters. Bronze knives and spoons. (*Pompeii.*)

CABINET LIX.,

76543. Large EGG FRAME, capable of cooking twenty-nine eggs at once. (*Inn, Pompeii.*)

76540. Very handsome ANDIRONS.

76542. Egg-frame for four eggs. (*Pompeii.*)

Seven SPITS. (*Pompeii.*)

76540–1. TWO TRIVETS, with bulls' heads and sea-horses. (Very fine.) (*Pompeii.*)

Tart dishes, frying-pans, gridirons, tongs, artistic fire-shovels, kitchen trivets. An iron TRIVET, much oxidized and covered with *lapilli*, with a pot firmly stuck to it by the oxidization.

Hanging up against the wall near the door,

78622. A bronze BELL, shaped like a gong. It has a beautiful tone, which may be heard by swinging the tongue which hangs before it. It was used at the end of the narrow streets where two vehicles could not pass, to warn people that a car was coming. (*Pompeii.*)

THE CABINET OF GEMS.

That artists who could work in metal as we have seen the Greeks could, should excel in the craft of the goldsmith, must be a matter of small surprise; at the same time we are hardly prepared to find gold ornaments and silver plate executed with a taste and finish to which we cannot arrive in our day with all our wealth and all our appliances.

The mention of Joseph's silver cup (Gen. xliv. 2) shows us how early in the history of the world the precious metals were used for the purposes for which we now adopt them, and as early as the time of Abraham we find mention made of the golden ear-ring (Gen. xxiv. 22) which Eleazar presented to Rebekah, though as it is spoken of in the singular number, and is mentioned as weighing half a shekel, we may assume the marginal reading of "jewel for the forehead" to be the more correct one.

The variety of purposes for which gold and silver ornaments were used as early as B.C. 750 appears in an interesting passage of Scripture (Isaiah iii. 18) which recites nearly all the articles of jewellery exhibited in the beautiful collection before us, though it is scarcely likely that in the time of the prophet so high a perfection of work was attained. Considering that the precious metals have always preserved their value and been the standard, the subsequent decadence of the art is more to be wondered at, for until the time of the Italian Renaissance we find but meagre traces either of gold, silver, or cameos of any great worth or importance.

This collection contains some Greek cameos and intaglios of world-wide fame; it includes also a large number of fine mediæval gems.

The question whether or not the ancients had magnifying glasses wherewith to cut these gems is still uncertain (see No. 27,613, p. 33), but it seems impossible that the naked eye could attain to such minute exactitude. We know from Pliny that they could not cut the diamond, but when by any means one got broken we find they set a high value on the splinters, because they found that by their aid they could cut any other stone with great ease.

There are constant references in the classical writers to the decoration of cups and articles of furniture with gems and cameos, and their use for rings is of the highest antiquity.

The first mention of a ring in the Bible is in Gen. xxxviii. 18, where Judah gave his signet to Tamar, and again (Gen. xli. 42) where Pharaoh puts his ring on the hand of Joseph to invest him with authority; and indeed, without interruption throughout the history of the world, the "giving and receiving of a ring" has been the token of a solemn compact between the contracting parties. They were also frequently used much as we use letters of introduction, and given for this purpose to ambassadors and other high functionaries, and, as in the case of Hannibal, they frequently contained a dose of poison to enable their wearer to extricate himself from an unpleasant dilemma by an heroic suicide (see No. 157, p. 35).

ARTICLES OF GOLD.

24606. BULLÆ PATRITIÆ. Two gold bullæ with gold-wire loops to hang them round the neck by. They were worn by young patricians till they attained the age of seventeen years, when they were exchanged for the *toga virilis*, hung up in the house, and dedicated to the Lares. Amulets were placed in the hollow of them, to bring good luck and keep off evil spirits. (*Herculaneum.*)

Sundry necklaces of beads, links, and precious stones. Well-wrought gold braid, ear-rings, trinkets, and rings set with fine stones, of which 24732-3-4 still contain the finger-bones of their owners. (*Pompeii.*)

25813. Amber statuette with cloak and wig. (*P.*)

†27613. A CIRCULAR PIECE OF GLASS, thought to be a magnifying glass. This unique specimen has given rise to much discussion, the received opinion being that it is a lens, a point that cannot be satisfactorily proved unless it is repolished. On the other hand, we have no mention of any instrument of the kind, and many authorities assert that they were unknown to the ancients. (*Pompeii.*)

†25234 *et seq.* GREEK EAR-RINGS of large size and great beauty, with a sardonyx ring (the setting modern) bearing

D

an Amazon; and a gold coin from Syracuse, found in a tomb at Taranto. (*Gift of Baron d'Arbou-Castillon, 1864.*)

*Magnificent specimens of gold work found in the upper story of a house at Pompeii in November 1870, comprising the largest gold chain yet found; bracelets, a necklace, and several pairs of ear-rings, set with fine emeralds and pearls.

†25000. Large gold lamp, without a cover (weighing 896 grammes, nearly 2 pounds avoirdupois), and having its handle formed of a leaf. It is in the most perfect preservation, and is the only gold lamp as yet found in Pompeii. Probably a votive offering to Pallas. (1863.)

Among sundry other gold ornaments,

*24825. Two bracelets in the form of serpents—the largest known—weight two pounds. (*House of the Faun, Pompeii.*)

24826. KID in solid gold, from Edessa in Mesopotamia. (*Borgia.*)

24833. Superb necklace of gold chain, ornamented with boss and pendent vine-leaves.

24845–6. Two large *fibulæ* or pin clasps, from which hang two pomegranates that do not belong to them. (*Pompeii.*)

†24852. SOLID GOLD BULL, bearing inscriptions in Phœnician and in Greek. It was found at Syracuse, and no doubt was connected with the worship of Apis (Ex. xxxii. 19).

†24883. MAGNIFICENT NECKLACE, the finest in the collection, ornamented with 21 masks of Silenus and 58 ornamental acorns and *fleurs de lys.* Found in the *Vase of Triptolemus.*

24893. Superb diadem set with precious stones (from a Greek tomb at *Venosa*).

24876 and –8. Two blue glass bottles in gold stands of exquisite designs. They probably contained perfumes, and were found in a tomb at Venosa.

†Sundry beautiful necklaces, clasps, and trinkets. (*Pompeii* and *Herculaneum.*)

110834. Lady's hair-net, made of gold wire. (*Pompeii.*)

Sundry engraved amethysts, topazes, emeralds, &c., recently found. (*Pompeii.*)

THE RINGS.

Many are set with fine stones and emerald plasmas, and the majority came from either Herculaneum or Pompeii.

Double rings, made of two united circles. It is asserted that these were wedding rings. Some of them have an anchor and a palm in the place of the setting.

Rings made in imitation of serpents.

†501, *red no.* Very large ring, which was probably used for a seal, having a well-cut *head of Brutus.* It bears in Greek letters, written from right to left, "*Anaxilas made me.*" Weight, three ounces.

136, *red no.* Ring bearing the name of the owner, "Cassia," found on the finger of a skeleton in the House of the Faun, with two bracelets (see No. 24825, p. 34), and several ear-rings, a jewel-case, gold coins, &c.

†157, *red no.* Ring set with an emerald plasma of convex form, intended to hold poison.

161, *red no.* Necklace ornaments, representing three Egyptian figures in glass.

179, *red no.* Ring with a cameo representing a theatrical mask, found at Pompeii by King Charles III. When he left Naples for Spain, he deposited it in the Museum.

TAZZA FARNESE.

In the window,

*Cup of Oriental sardonyx, known as the *Tazza Farnese.* The intrinsic value of this *tazza* is inestimable, and its artistic merit renders it unique. It is said to have been found at *Rome* in the *Mausoleum of Hadrian,* now called the *Castle Sant' Angelo;* but it seems more probable that it was found in the ruins of Hadrian's villa by a soldier, who gave it to the Duke Charles of Bourbon when he was besieging Rome. Unfortunately, prior to its reaching the Farnese Collection, its owner caused a hole to be bored in the centre, that a foot might be fitted to it.

This incomparable relic has been the subject of many discussions among *savans,* and articles have been published about it by Maffei, Winckelmann, and others.

It is the only known cameo of its size which presents

a composition on each side. On the outer part is a magnificent Medusa's head, which covers it completely, and
on the inside are eight figures in relief which stand out
against the dark background.

Archæologists are not agreed as to their explanation of
the subject. The interpretation which seems to us the
most probable is that of Comm. Quaranta, who explains
it as *Ptolemy Philadelphia consecrating the harvest festival
instituted by Alexander the Great, after the foundation of
Alexandria.*

Egypt is represented by the Sphinx, at whose right
sits *Isis* holding an ear of corn. The old man in the upper
section, with his back against a fig-tree, is probably the
Nile, holding an empty cornucopia, the symbol of great
rivers; and below the Nile hover two youths, who per-
sonify the Etesian winds, whose breath arrests the course
of the Nile and fertilizes Egypt.

The two nymphs seated on the right, one holding an
empty horn and the other a cup, are nymphs of the Nile,
protectresses of Egypt.

And finally the figure which occupies the centre of the
composition is one of the *Ptolemies*, with the attributes of
Horus-Apollo, a chief Egyptian divinity and son of Isis,
holding an hydraulic instrument for measuring the inunda-
tion of the Nile, and a dagger.

ARTICLES OF SILVER PLATE.

25284. THREE ALTARS, of which two are alike, while the
third is a little smaller and set with rubies. They are of four
pilasters, with bronze plinths surmounted by a *cortina* or
bowl, and ornamented with graceful foliage. (*Rome.*)

†25289. Silver pail with bronze handle. Around it a
portico in bas-relief; on one side five nude women issuing
from the baths hard by,—one is seated, the others are
waiting upon her. On the other side are three nude
women near a fountain, one of whom is opening the door
of the baths, while another is dressing the third. (*H.*)

†25301. APOTHEOSIS OF HOMER. A mortar-shaped cup
with the above design in bas-relief. This is one of the
most celebrated pieces of silver plate that has come down
to us from the ancients.

The poet is clothed in the *Vestis talaris*, and his head half veiled; he is borne heavenwards by an eagle. On the left the Iliad personified, armed *cap-à-pie*, and wearing the *chiton* and the *perones*. On the right the Odyssey with the *pileus*, and her head resting on her right hand. (*H.*)

25343. Silver censer with cover and chain. (*Rome.*)

Sundry beautiful cups, saucers, dishes, eleven saucepans, mortar, &c. (*Pompeii* and *Herculaneum.*)

*25367. A cup with bas-relief of Apollo in his car. (*P.*)

†25376 *et seq.* Six beautiful cups adorned with bas-reliefs and lined to prevent deposit in the concavities. The designs relate to the worship of Bacchus. (*Pompeii.*)

109688. Exquisite silver skeleton. (1873. *Pompeii.*)

111760. Statuette in a bronze chair, completely oxidized. (*Pompeii.*)

25382-3. Statuettes of a Camillus and of Abundance. (*Pompeii.*)

109661. A flat spoon of very elegant design.

25498. Hairpin. Venus and Cupid.

25488. Two Genii dancing to the *tibia*.

25489. ABUNDANCE; a round *plaque* in perfect preservation. (*Pompeii.*)

25490. The reverse of a circular mirror representing the death of Cleopatra. The queen is sitting, having just been bitten by the asp, her head supported by an attendant. Below the chair is the basket of figs in which Plutarch tells us that Cleopatra's two attendants, Charmion and Eiras, hid the asp. (*Pompeii.*)

†25492-3. Diana and Apollo. Two oval high reliefs. (*Herculaneum.*)

†25494. BRONZE SUN-DIAL, faced with silver, in the shape of a ham. The hours are indicated by vertical lines, beneath which are the names of the months. The knuckle served as a gnomon. This is believed to be the only ancient portable sun-dial extant. (*Herculaneum.*)

25495. Circular bas-relief of a Satyr playing the lyre before a hermes. (*Herculaneum.*)

109331. Apollo seated beneath a tree, with a snake twined round his staff. (1872. *Pompeii.*)

Sundry rings, bracelets, cups, shapes, and fragments. (*Pompeii* and *Herculaneum.*)

25496. A delicate silver colander. (*Herculaneum.*)

Eight pitchers (*lagenæ*), a round plate, a large rectangular plate, goblets, spoons with their own cups, arm-
lets, a systrum, some mirrors, two strigils, and a handsome *unguentarium* with removable cup; some beautiful
silver dishes, and sundry fragments. (*P.* and *H.*)·

In the glazed tables,

CAMEOS AND INTAGLIOS.

This collection comprises about a thousand cameos and
five hundred intaglios, many of **which** bear the name of
Lorenzo dei Medici, and came from **the Farnese** Collection.
The remainder are from Pompeii **and** Herculaneum.
The ancient specimens are marked " **Ant.***," and the mediæval*
***ones* "** xv." (*fifteenth century*).

FIRST TABLE.—FIRST COMPARTMENT (*next window*).

25833 to 25899.

FIRST ROW,

1. *Onyx.* THE EDUCATION OF BACCHUS. The infant god,
mounted on a lion led by a nymph, is held up by one of
the *Nysiades;* behind, *Nysa* seated. *Ant.*

2. *Onyx.* MELEAGER, sitting and **caressing his** dog;
two women in conversation. *Ant.*

3. *Onyx.* A NEREID on a Triton, playing cymbals. *Ant.*

4. *Sardonyx.* VENUS surprised at her bath. *Ant.*

5. *Onyx.* NEPTUNE **and** PALLAS disputing about the
name to be given to a rising city. Inscribed ΠΥ—probably meaning *Pyrgotele.* **Ant.**

6. *Onyx.* DÆDALUS and ICARUS. Two females admiring
the prodigy—probably **Pasiphaë and Diana** Dyctine—per-
sonifying the Cretan city. **Ant.**

7. *Onyx.* VENUS on a lion **led by Cupid.** *Ant.*

8. *Oriental Onyx.* TRIUMPH OF BACCHUS and SILENUS.
The car is drawn by two Psyches, the reins held by
Cupid, while another pushes the car. *Ant.*

9. *Onyx.* BEAR-HUNT. Inscribed GNEIUS. *Ant.*

SECOND ROW,

10. *Sardonyx.* TWO FEMALE HEADS. *Ant.*

11. *Onyx.* Faun and Bacchante. *Ant.*
12. *Onyx.* CHARIOT driven by VICTORY. Legend, ΣΟΣΤΡΑΤΟΥ. *Ant.*
13. *Agate.* HELLE on a ram, and Cupid. xv.
14. *Oriental Onyx.* Male and female CENTAUR. *Ant.*
*16. *Onyx.* JUPITER overwhelming the *Titans.* Legend, ΑΘΗΝΙΩΝ. *Ant.*
17. *Onyx.* COCK-FIGHT, in presence of two Cupids, one lamenting his defeat, the other victorious. *Ant.*
18. *Onyx.* HERCULES and OMPHALE. *Ant.*
19. *Sardonyx.* HEAD of OMPHALE. *Ant.*
20. *Onyx.* BACCHUS finding Ariadne. *Ant.*
21. *Oriental Onyx.* CUPIDS at work. *Ant.*

THIRD ROW,

23. *Agate.* ULYSSES at rest. xv.
24. *Sardonyx.* A ROMAN LADY; portrait. *Ant.*
25. *Sardonyx.* HOMER; name on the mantle. *Ant.*
26. *Onyx.* NYMPHS sporting with Cupids on a tree. *Ant.*
27. *Agate.* A NEREID on the *hippocampus.* *Ant.*
28. *Agate.* AURORA in a *biga.* *Ant.*
29. *Onyx.* OMPHALE with the club of Hercules. *Ant.*
†30. *Agate.* JUPITER SERAPIS, in high relief. *Ant.*
31. *Onyx.* HERCULES bearing Cupid. *Ant.*
32. *Agate.* Head of MEDUSA. *Ant.*
33. *Agate.* SATYR kneeling. A fragment. *Ant.*
34. *Agate.* TWO COMBATANTS. *Ant.*
35. *Onyx.* BACCHANTE playing the *tibia.* *Ant.*
36. *Agate.* Head of HERCULES, with a fillet. *Ant.*
37. *Onyx.* SATYR and BACCHANTE. xv.

FOURTH ROW,

38. *Agate.* OTHRYADES dying. *Ant.*

Othryades was the only survivor of 300 Spartans who fought 300 Argives for Thyrea. He returned to the camp, raised a trophy, wrote *vici* with his own blood on his shield, and killed himself, unwilling to survive the death of his comrades.

39. *Sardonyx on glass.* Head of Medusa. *Ant.*
40. *Sardonyx.* MALE HEAD, crowned. *Ant.*
†41. *Sardonyx.* SATYR dancing. A fragment. *Ant.*
42. *Agate.* MINERVA with helmet and quiver. *Ant.*
43. *Sardonyx.* Head of MINERVA. *Ant.*

†44. *Sardonyx.* Augustus. Attributed to *Dioscorides.*

45. *Glass.* Head of Mercury. xv.

46. *Onyx.* Genius running with a palm branch. *Ant.*

†47. *Onyx.* Aurora in her chariot. *Ant.*

†48. *Oriental Onyx.* A Faun carrying the infant Bacchus. *Ant.*

49. *Agate.* Female **head.** xv.

50. *Agate.* Genius of Bacchus on a ram. xv.

Fifth row,

51. **Onyx.** Satyr and Faun. **A** fragment. *Ant.*

52. *Onyx.* A fine head, perhaps Cicero. *Ant.*

53. *Onyx.* Victory, on a *biga.* xv.

54. *Onyx.* Three Cupids playing with a ram. **xv.**

55. *Oriental Onyx.* Venus and Cupid.

56. *Onyx.* Faun and Bacchante. ***Ant.***

†57. *Sardonyx.* Centaur. *Ant.*

58. *Sardonyx.* Bellerophon killing a lion. *Ant.*

59. *Sardonyx.* Venus sitting with Cupid on **her** knees. xv.

†60. *Oriental Onyx.* Sculptor chiselling a vase. *Ant.*

61. *Oriental Onyx.* Nereid on *hippocampus.* *Ant.*

62. *Agate.* Bust of a woman. xv.

63. *Oriental Onyx.* Silenus on a fawn's skin. *Ant.*

Sixth row,

64. *Agate.* Two Egyptian birds. *Ant.*

65. *Agate.* Dirce's punishment. Fragment.

66. *White and red Onyx.* Egyptian bird. *Ant.*

Seventh row,

1857. **Onyx enamelled.** Vestal, a superb head. *Ant.*

SECOND COMPARTMENT.

25900 to 26042.

First row,

67. *Onyx.* Silenus near an altar. *Ant.*

68. *Sardonyx.* A man's head, perhaps Mæcenas. *Ant.*

69. *Agate.* Ariobarzanus III., king of Cappadocia (?). *Ant.*

72. *Onyx.* Chariot. xv.

75. *Agate.* Priest of Bacchus. *Ant.*

76. *Sardonyx.* BACCHANTE. **xv.**
77. *Sardonyx.* DOMITIAN, laurel-crowned. **xv.**
78. *Agate.* FAUSTINA the younger (?). *Ant.*
79. *Sardonyx.* CUPID and PSYCHE. *Ant.*
83. *Onyx.* MINERVA. **xv.**
84. *Agate.* A CHILD'S HEAD. *Ant.*
85. *Sardonyx.* Bust of MINERVA. *Ant.*
86. *Onyx.* HERCULES strangling the serpents. *Ant.*
87. *Agate.* CASSANDRA at the *Palladium.* **xv.**

SECOND ROW,

88. *Oriental Onyx.* CENTAUR playing the *tibia.* *Ant.*
90. *Sapphire.* Veiled **head** of LIVIA. **xv.**
93. **Emerald.** Lotus-crowned head of ISIS. *Ant.*
97. **Agate.** AJAX dragging Cassandra from the *Palladium.* **Ant.**
99. *Lapis-lazuli.* **Tiberius** crowned with laurel. **xv.**
100. *Agate.* VICTORY, in a *biga.* *Ant.*
105. *Emerald.* Bust of JUPITER SERAPIS. **Ant.**
108. *Chrysolite.* HARPOCRATES. **xv.**

THIRD ROW,

112. *Sardonyx.* SILENUS with a snake round his arm. **xv.**
120. *Sardonyx.* Bust of a PHILOSOPHER. **xv.**
123. *Jacinth.* CLEOPATRA. **xv.**
124. *Onyx.* MARSYAS bound and MERCURY. **Ant.**
130. **Agate.** JUBA II., king of Mauritania. **Ant.**
131. **Jade.** Bust of a CHILD. **Ant.**
133. **Agate** (*modern*). Head of NERO. **xv.**
134. **Onyx.** LEDA and the SWAN. **Ant.**

FOURTH ROW,

138. *Onyx.* SACRIFICE TO PRIAPUS. *Ant.*
139. *Agate.* CUPIDS with lyre and panpipe. **Ant.**
147. *Sardonyx.* HERCULES and the lion. **xv.**
152. *Onyx.* CUPID on a car drawn by goats. **Ant.**
154. *Onyx.* GANYMEDE and THE EAGLE. **xv.**
156. **Agate.** Hercules with the lion's skin. **xv.**

FIFTH ROW,

158. *Agate.* THREE CUPIDS forging darts. *Ant.*
160. *Onyx.* VENUS and MARS. *Ant.*
161. *Oriental Onyx.* LIVIA as JUNO. *Ant.*
164. **Onyx.** CUPID leaning on his torch. **Ant.**

167. *Garnet.* SAMSON, with legend. xv.
171. *Agate.* DOMITIAN. xv.
172. *Agate.* Head of JULIA MÆSA. *Ant.*
175. *Onyx.* Bust of AQUILA SEVERA? *Ant.*
176. *Agate.* Bust of JULIA SŒMIS? *Ant.*

SIXTH ROW,

185. *Onyx.* Head of AGRIPPINA. *Ant.*
†188. *Sardonyx.* AURORA on a *quadriga.* The artist knew how to make the most of the different strata of the stone to give each horse a distinct colour. According to Winckelmann, their colours indicate dawn, day, twilight, and night. *Ant.*
190. *Onyx.* ERATO playing the lyre. *Ant.*
193. *Onyx.* CUPID; legend—ΦΙΛΩ, *I love. Ant.*
196. *Jacinth Chrysopath.* CÆSAR. xv.
197. *Onyx.* Hand pulling an ear; MNHMONEYE— *remember. Ant.*
198. *Onyx.* Hand-in-hand; OMONOIA, *concord. Ant.*
199. *Onyx.* CUPID leaning on his torch. *Ant.*

SEVENTH ROW,

201. *Onyx.* GANYMEDE borne by the eagle. *Ant.*
†203. *Agate.* THETIS on a dolphin, with Triton and Zephyr. xv.
206. *Glass.* Tiberius. (*Pompeii.*)

INTAGLIOS.

26043 to 26209.

SECOND TABLE—FIRST COMPARTMENT.

FIRST ROW,

205. *Amethyst.* OLD MAN, with cloak. *Ant.*
206. *Garnet.* VESTAL. *Ant.*
207. *Sardonyx.* THE HERACLIDÆ drawing lots. *Ant.*
†209. *Cornelian.* AJAX and Cassandra at the Palladium. *Ant.*
210. *Chalcedony.* Head of infant HERCULES. xv.
212. *Emerald Plasma.* ORPHEUS playing the lyre. *Ant.*
213. *Cornelian.* APOLLO and MARSYAS bound. *Ant.*
†214. *Chrysolite.* PALLAS. xv.

†215. *Chalcedony*. ANTONINUS PIUS (?). **xv.**

216. *Sardonyx*. Bust of JULIA. **xv.**

219. *Cornelian*. PERSEUS with the **head** of *Medusa*. Legend—ΔIOΣK... Dioscorides. *Ant.*

221. *Cornelian*. SOLON. Legend—ΣΟΛΩΝΟΣ. *Ant.*

SECOND ROW,

226. *Cornelian*. SILENUS with Faun and Bacchante. *Ant.*

227. *Green Plasma*. CUPID drawn by butterflies. *Ant.*

228. *Amethyst*. JOLE; a fine head. **xv.**

229. *Cornelian*. THETIS and a Triton. *Ant.*

230. *Sapphire*. Fine bust of JUNO. *Ant.*

231. *Cornelian*. Head of MARCUS AURELIUS. *Ant.*

*232. *Amethyst*. DIANA, with Apollonius inscribed in Greek. A gem of great celebrity. *Ant.*

233. *Cornelian*. Head of PHILOSOPHER. *Ant.*

†234. *Chalcedony*. ACTOR with a mask. **xv.**

236. *Agate*. SABINE. **xv.**

238. *Cornelian*. Head of ANTINOUS. *Ant.*

THIRD ROW,

244. *Beryl*. Head of SERGIUS GALBA. **xv.**

247. *Amethyst*. MOUNTED WARRIOR. *Ant.*

248. *Cornelian*. THE CAR OF THE SUN. *Ant.*

250. *Amethyst*. ANTONINUS PIUS. *Ant.*

251. *Sardonyx*. TRAJAN and his wife PLOTINA, MARCIANA his sister, and his niece MATIDIA. Group. *Ant.*

253. *Amethyst*. THETIS on two sea-horses. *Ant.*

254. *Cornelian*. PERSEUS with Medusa's head. Inscribed *Dioscorides*. *Ant.*

256. *Cornelian*. HADRIAN, crowned. *Ant.*

260. Head of PTOLEMY PHILADELPHIA. *Ant.*

FOURTH ROW,

266. *Cornelian*. THESEUS and the Minotaur. *Ant.*

268. *Cornelian*. Fine head of PLATO. **xv.**

276. *Cornelian*. JULIUS CÆSAR. **xv.**

279. *Garnet*. HARPOCRATES. *Ant.*

FIFTH ROW,

287. *Garnet*. Bust of CLEOPATRA. *Ant.*

Sixth row,

The *first* stone, without a number.

Cornelian. Handsome bust of Juno. (*Pompeii.*)

Seventh row,

329. *Sardonyx.* Mars crowned by Victory. *Ant.*

Ninth row,

362. *Cornelian.* Pallas bearing an image of Victory. *Ant.*

369. *Green Plasma.* Marcus Aurelius. *Ant.*

SECOND COMPARTMENT.

26210 to 26389.

First row,

372. *Green Jasper.* Head of a Philosopher. xv.

373. *Sardonyx.* Woman's head. xv.

Second row,

†390. *Cornelian.* Sacrifice. Group of 18 figures. xv.

392. *Cornelian.* Woman on a couch. *Ant.*

393. *Agate.* Plotina, a fine head. xv.

404. *Heliotrope Jasper.* Æsculapius. xv.

408. *Cornelian.* Silenus upon an ass. Group. xv.

Third row,

413. *Cornelian.* Pescennius, with inscription. xv.

414. *Cornelian.* Apollo with Minerva, playing the lyre. xv.

417. *Sanguine Jasper.* Sacrifice. xv.

419. *Cornelian.* Livia and Tiberius. Group. xv.

Fourth row,

428. *Cornelian.* Julia, daughter of *Titus.* xv.

431. *Lapis-lazuli.* Mars, standing. xv.

438. *Sardonyx.* Vulcan, with his forge. xv.

439. *Cornelian.* Strength conquered by Beauty. A woman seated on a lion, with two Cupids. Legend— ΑΛΕΞΑΝ... "Alexander." xv.

Fifth row,

445. *Green Jasper.* Bacchante, with thyrsus and cornu copia. *Ant.*

446. *Cornelian.* Cupid drawing water. xv.

451. *Emerald Plasma.* JUPITER, JUNO, and MINERVA. *Ant.*
455. *Sardonyx.* CUPID dedicating one wing to the Sun. xv.

SIXTH ROW,
  473. *Chalcedony.* AFRICA PERSONIFIED. Engraved with unintelligible characters. *Ant.*
  474. *Agate.* GALBA crowned with laurel. xv.

SEVENTH ROW,
  490. *Chalcedony.* VICTORY. *Ant.*
  494. *Sardonyx.* THEATRICAL MASK. *Ant.*
  503. *Agate.* DOLPHIN. xv.

EIGHTH ROW,
  521. *Topaz.* HIPPOCAMPUS. xv.
  524. *Jade.* A handsome female head. *Ant.*
  †531. *Lapis-lazuli.* Galerius Maximinus. xv.

OTHER INTAGLIOS AND CAMEOS.

THIRD TABLE—FIRST COMPARTMENT.

26390 to 26766.

(INTAGLIOS.)

FIRST ROW,
  573. *Cornelian.* Head of CYBELE. *Ant.*

SECOND ROW,
  584. *Chalcedony.* JUPITER enthroned. xv.
  589. *Cornelian.* VULCAN forging thunderbolts. xv.
  †592. *Cornelian.* MARS in full armour. *Ant.*

THIRD ROW,
  607. *Cornelian.* PRIAM and one of his soldiers. *Ant.*
  617. *Cornelian.* PROTESILAUS and LAODAMIA (?) *Ant.*
  620. *Sardonyx.* VICTORY on a chariot. *Ant.*

FOURTH ROW,
  641. *Plasma.* Three divinities in a temple. *Ant.*
  644. *Green Jasper.* JUPITER SERAPIS and JUNO. *Ant.*

FIFTH ROW,
  659. *Cornelian.* WARRIOR putting on his cuirass. *Ant.*
  679. *Sardonyx.* CUPID before Priapus. *Ant.*

Sixth row,

691. *Cornelian.* Fortune. *Ant.*
695. *Sardonyx.* Minerva. *Ant.*

Seventh row,

726. *Cornelian.* Pegasus. *Ant.*

Eighth row,

779. *Cornelian.* Minerva crowned by Victory. *Ant.*

Ninth row,

884. *Cyprian Jasper.* Household god. *Ant.*
905. *Emerald Plasma.* Satire personified. *Ant.*

SECOND COMPARTMENT.:

26767 to 26965.

(Cameos.)

First row,

930. *Agate.* Fine female bust. *Ant.*
931. *Agate.* Minerva, with helmet. *Ant.*
933. *Turquoise.* Sabina ; bust, with head of Medusa. *Ant.*

Second row,

940. *Onyx.* Negro's head. *Ant.*
946. *Agate.* Pretty portrait of a woman. xv.

Third row,

961. **Agate.** Minerva, fully armed. Bust. xv.
967. *Onyx.* Aurora in her chariot. *Ant.*
969. **Glass.** Commodus (?). Bust. *Ant.*

Fourth row,

988. *Onyx.* The Three Graces. xv.
992. *Onyx.* Orpheus. *Ant.*

Fifth row,

1003. *Onyx.* Minerva. xv.

Sixth row,

†1021. *Lapis-lazuli.* Minerva armed. xv.
†1024. *Onyx.* Alexander the Great. xv

Seventh row,

1044. *Onyx.* Mæcenas ? xv.
1046. *Agate.* Socrates. xv.

FOURTH TABLE.

(This table contains sundry specimens of less interest.)

1129. *Agate.* Thetis on a Triton. *Ant.*
1162. *Agate.* Head of Cicero. KI-KE-PO. *Ant.*
1217. Large scarabæus. *Ant.*
A necklace of scarabæi.
1375. *Green Jasper.* Aurora. xv.
†1452. *Cornelian.* A *bulla* mounted with gold wire to hang round the neck, representing a man and his wife—probably portraits of the wearer's parents. *Ant.*

LAST TABLE.

27349 to 27610.

PORTRAITS in intaglio, designed as *ornaments for necklaces.*
1520. *Sardonyx.* JUPITER. Bust. xv.
1540. *Shell-fish.* Three Cupids drawing water. xv.
1559. *Sardonyx.* An eagle. xv.
From 1701 to 1703. *Agates.* Vases for perfume. *Ant.*
Agate. A "knucklebone." *Ant.*
Two large RINGS belonging to Cardinals of the Farnese family. They are silver-gilt.

LONDON: PRINTED BY WILLIAM CLOWES AND SONS, LIMITED,
STAMFORD STREET AND CHARING CROSS.

www.ingramcontent.com/pod-product-compliance
Lightning Source LLC
Chambersburg PA
CBHW021644270326
41931CB00008B/1154